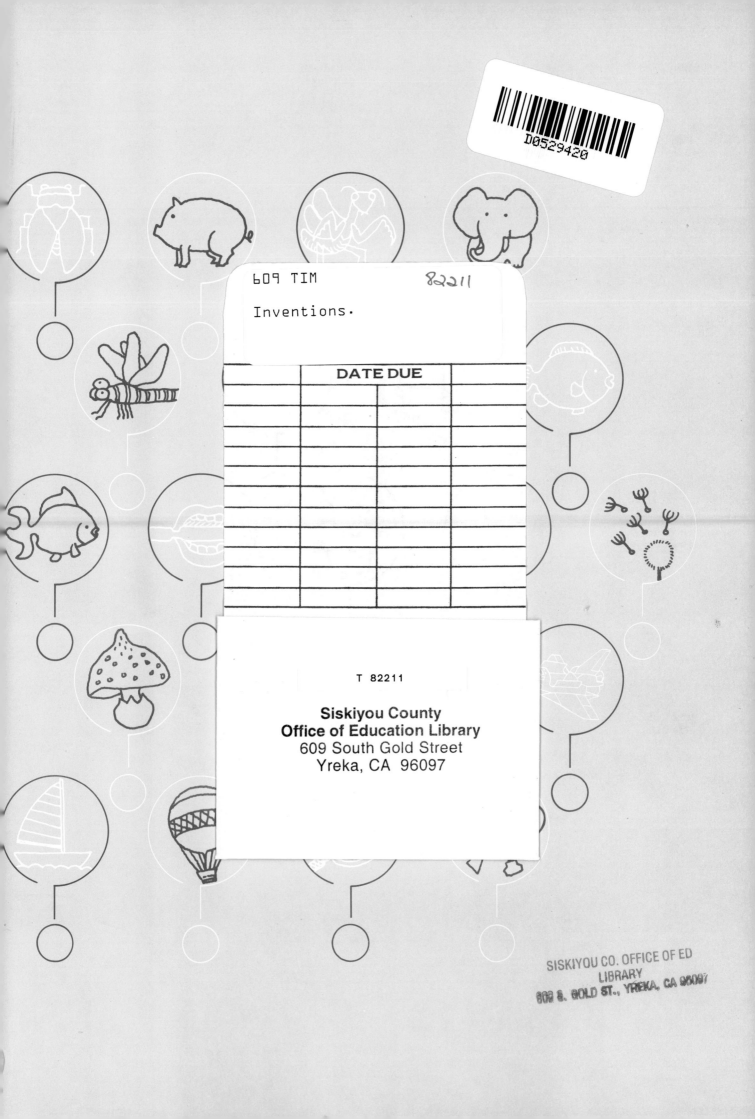

609 TIM   82211

Inventions.

	DATE DUE		

A Child's First Library of Learning

Inventions

TIME-LIFE BOOKS • ALEXANDRIA, VIRGINIA

Contents

❓ What's an Invention?

ANSWER When someone has an idea for something new and makes it work, it is called an invention. Sometimes many people work on an idea together. At other times one person begins and several people improve the invention.

Inventions on demand

■ First canned food

In 1795, when Napoléon Bonaparte led the French army, he looked for ways to keep food from spoiling. His soldiers needed food that would not go bad on long marches. Nicolas-François Appert had an idea. He boiled food in glass jars to kill any germs and sealed the jars with cork so no new germs could get in.

■ The phonograph

In the United States, Thomas Edison often tried to make machines work in new ways. In 1877, when he tested the telegraph, he heard the machine's needle repeat a message at high speed, making a sound like music. Edison suddenly realized that he could record sounds' vibrations as electrical pulses and later change them back into sounds. And that was the idea for the phonograph.

Inventions by chance

▼ The first words Edison recorded on his phonograph were "Mary had a little lamb."

● **To the Parent**

When Edison invented the phonograph, he meant to produce a device that would record telephone messages. His mind was "filled with theories of sound vibrations and their transmissions by diaphragms," he said. When he experimented with the stylus and tape of a telegraph machine, he noticed that the tape produced sounds as the stylus read the impressions at high speed. He discovered that he could convert the vibrations of sound into electric impulses and back into sound. During his lifetime, Edison had so many ideas that he obtained 1,093 patents for inventions.

Which Inventions Have Changed the World?

ANSWER Sometimes an invention is so important, it changes forever the way people do their work. Paper and the steam engine made such a difference. Paper was invented 2,000 years ago in China. Until then people wrote on thin strips of papyrus stems or carved messages in stone or wood. Scotsman James Watt developed the steam engine in 1765. The machine could do heavy work in factories that people had done before by hand.

▲ In ancient Egypt people wrote on thin strips of papyrus stems that were joined together.

■ Invention of paper

Paper was first made in China in A.D. 105. A papermaker began by boiling raw plant fiber like hemp or cotton until the fiber turned to mush. He spread the mush on a screen in a wood frame and soaked the mush in water. When he lifted the frame out of the water to drain, only a thin film of mush was left. As the film dried, it became a sheet of paper.

■ The steam engine

In 1765, when most work was done by hand, engineer James Watt improved a steam engine that had been invented by Thomas Newcomen. Watt's engine could turn cranks and rollers in factories and do work faster than people could. Factory smokestacks soon were billowing smoke as the engines burned coal to make the steam that powered machines. The machines produced goods like fabrics and did heavy work in mines. The engines also powered ships and trains, carrying goods and people faster than before.

The steamboat "Clermont"

The steam locomotive "Rocket"

● To the Parent

Watt's improvement of the steam engine led to the development of steam locomotives and steamships, which made transportation easier. The steam engine also helped usher in England's Industrial Revolution by making it possible for industry to shift from manual labor to machine power. This single invention dramatically changed the world we live in.

What Led to the Invention of the Printing Press?

ANSWER After the invention of paper, people found different ways to write on it. Some wrote with pen and ink. Others carved a message in a block of wood, brushed the wood with ink, and pressed it against paper. In 1438 the German silversmith Johannes Gutenberg thought of making letters that could be used many times and rearranged to spell out any word. Gutenberg also built a machine, called a press, that could print a whole page at a time.

■ It began with a mistake

Gutenberg was carving out a message one day. He had almost reached the end of a line when he made a mistake. Instead of carving the whole line again, he cut out the wrong letter and replaced it with the right one. He realized that he did not have to redo all of his work to correct one mistake.

After Gutenberg thought of using movable letters for printing, he invented a machine to print *(right)*. Until then people had printed by hand. They laid the paper on inked letters and rubbed a heavy, flat stone across the paper to press it down and make a print. Gutenberg had the idea of changing a machine that had been used for pressing grapes into a machine that could press down evenly on paper. He called the machine a printing press. The machine could print much faster and more clearly than the old method.

■ How printing was invented

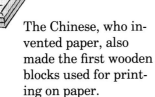

The Chinese, who invented paper, also made the first wooden blocks used for printing on paper.

? Who Invented the Light Bulb?

ANSWER Many people tried to make a light bulb, but no one could come up with one that glowed for more than a few seconds. The filament inside the bulb—the part that glows—burned up right away. Thomas Edison tried thousands of different materials for the filament. Finally, in 1879, he discovered that a carbon filament lasted longest. He used it in his light bulb, and it glowed for more than 13 hours.

■ First experiments

▲ One of Edison's early electric light bulbs glowed for only a few minutes. A platinum wire burned for a little more than one hour.

▲ Edison tested some 6,000 different materials to find a filament that would not burn up in seconds. In the end he found that a carbon filament would glow for many hours.

■ Another test

One of the materials Edison experimented with was a filament made of bamboo from a Japanese fan. It burned longer than many other kinds of plant matter, but the most successful filament was a carbon thread.

How Did We Get the Telephone?

ANSWER The sound of the human voice reaches our ears because of vibrations the sound sets up in the air. Scots-born Alexander Graham Bell tried to convert sound waves into electric impulses so they could be sent over great distances. After many trials, Bell made his experiment work in 1876. In his first telephone call, Bell said to his assistant, who was in the next room, "Come here, Watson. I want you."

■ The first telephone

■ How Bell won

Elisha Gray had built a telephone similar to Bell's. But Bell beat Gray by two hours in filing an application for his invention at the patent office. Today we know only Alexander Graham Bell as the inventor of the telephone.

■ Edison's improvements

In Bell's telephone the same part was used for speaking and listening. Edison improved this model by making a telephone with a mouthpiece and an earpiece. He continued to refine the phone so that sound could be heard more clearly.

● **To the Parent**

In Bell's telephone, vibrations of a metal reed transmitted the sound. An electromagnet converted the vibrations into electric current. The sound, now in the form of an electric current, moved along a cable to a receiver, where the same process in reverse converted the electric signals back into sounds. By filing his patent two hours after Bell, Elisha Gray missed getting credit for his invention. For more than a decade he waged a futile legal battle against Bell.

? How Was the Radio Invented?

ANSWER Radio began in 1895 as a wireless system designed by Guglielmo Marconi of Italy. This system could send only Morse code signals of dots and dashes, rather than sound. Inventors worked for another 11 years to develop radios that could broadcast the sound of the human voice and music.

■ First broadcast

The world's first radio broadcast in December 1906 was a Christmas program. Reginald Fessenden made the transmission from the Massachusetts coast. People on ships and shore could hear the program for 15 miles around.

■ SOS from the "Titanic"

In 1912, when the passenger liner Titanic hit an iceberg and began to sink, the radio operator sent a call for help, transmitting the letters SOS in Morse code. The call brought the ship Carpathia to the rescue and saved 700 passengers from drowning.

▲ Electric generator

Reginald Fessenden

▲ Vacuum tube radio detector

John Fleming

■ Invention of radio

John Ambrose Fleming invented a vacuum tube that could pick up radio waves electronically. The vacuum tube regulated the flow of electric current that was produced by the electric generator developed by Reginald Fessenden.

Who Built and Flew the First Airplane?

ANSWER The brothers Orville and Wilbur Wright built the first airplane that a person could fly and control. Using parts from their bicycle shop, they manufactured a gasoline engine that turned two propellers attached to the rear of the main wings. The pilot had to lie stretched out flat on his stomach to fly the plane.

■ **The Wright brothers' plane**

In 1903 the Wright brothers made the first successful flight near Kitty Hawk in North Carolina. After many trials and one crash, the plane called the *Flyer* flew 852 feet and stayed in the air for 59 seconds.

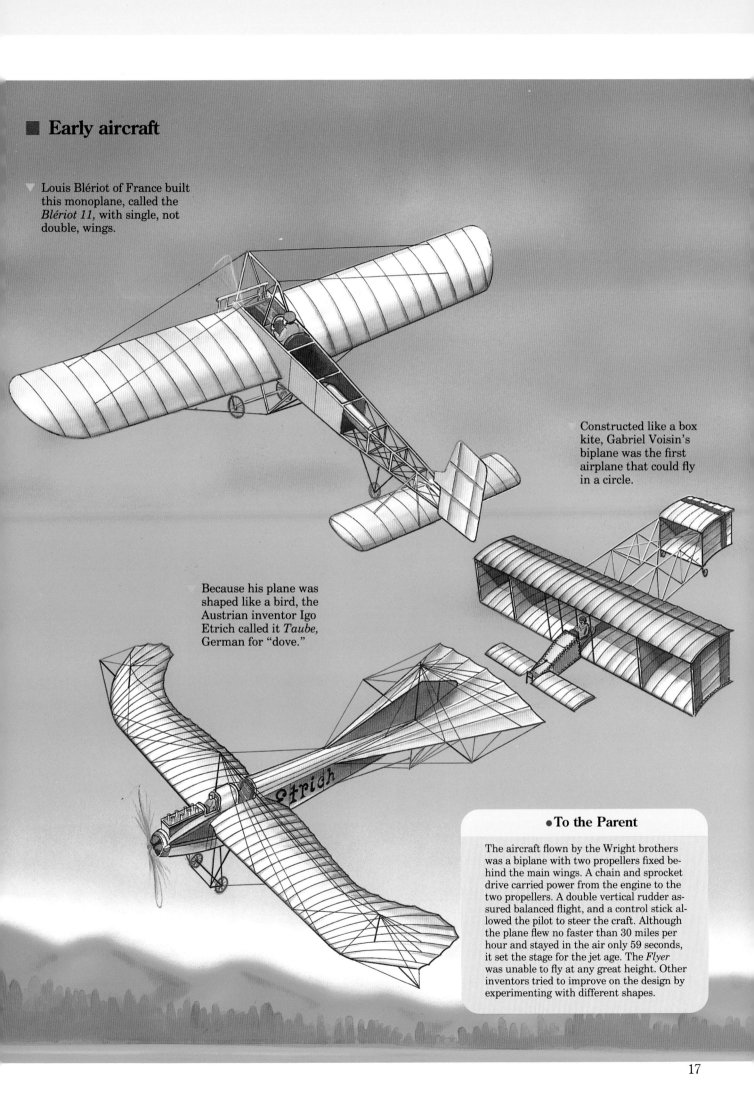

■ Early aircraft

▼ Louis Blériot of France built this monoplane, called the *Blériot 11,* with single, not double, wings.

Constructed like a box kite, Gabriel Voisin's biplane was the first airplane that could fly in a circle.

▼ Because his plane was shaped like a bird, the Austrian inventor Igo Etrich called it *Taube,* German for "dove."

● To the Parent

The aircraft flown by the Wright brothers was a biplane with two propellers fixed behind the main wings. A chain and sprocket drive carried power from the engine to the two propellers. A double vertical rudder assured balanced flight, and a control stick allowed the pilot to steer the craft. Although the plane flew no faster than 30 miles per hour and stayed in the air only 59 seconds, it set the stage for the jet age. The *Flyer* was unable to fly at any great height. Other inventors tried to improve on the design by experimenting with different shapes.

❓ Why Did the First Cars Look So Funny?

ANSWER The first automobile ever built had a big boiler in front. The boiler held water, which was heated until it turned into steam. The steam drove the car's engine. Years later cars were powered by gasoline, which could be held in small tanks, and the design of automobiles changed.

▲ The world's first automobile, built in 1769 by Nicolas-Joseph Cugnot of France, was driven by steam, not gasoline. This vehicle could go only a little faster than 2 miles per hour, slower than a person can walk.

■ Gasoline power

Called horseless carriages, the first automobiles to run on gasoline still looked much like carriages. The German engineer Gottlieb Daimler built the car shown at right, and Carl Benz manufactured the one below.

▲ **Daimler's four-wheeler (1889)**

◄ **Benz's tricycle (1886)**

The first popular car

In 1908 in the United States, Henry Ford manufactured a gasoline-powered automobile—called the Model T—that was affordable and easy to drive. Many people wanted to own one. The Model T was so popular that more than 15 million of the cars were sold worldwide between 1908 and 1927.

▲ Ford's quadricycle (1896)

The Model T Ford (1908)

● To the Parent

Carl Benz of Germany invented the first automobile with a gasoline-powered internal-combustion engine. Henry Ford developed his own model, standardized parts, and streamlined assembly so that he could sell an affordable car.

How Did the First Rocket Work?

(ANSWER) In 1926 Robert Hutchings Goddard launched the first liquid-fuel rocket in Auburn, Massachusetts. Powered by a mixture of gasoline and liquid oxygen as fuel, the rocket shot up into the air for 2.5 seconds. In its flight, the rocket went as high as 41 feet and came down 184 feet from the launch site.

The base of the rocket held two tanks, one filled with liquid oxygen and the other with gasoline. The fuels were combined and burned in a chamber with a nozzle at one end. As hot gases escaped through the nozzle, the rocket was propelled by the force of the exhaust pressure.

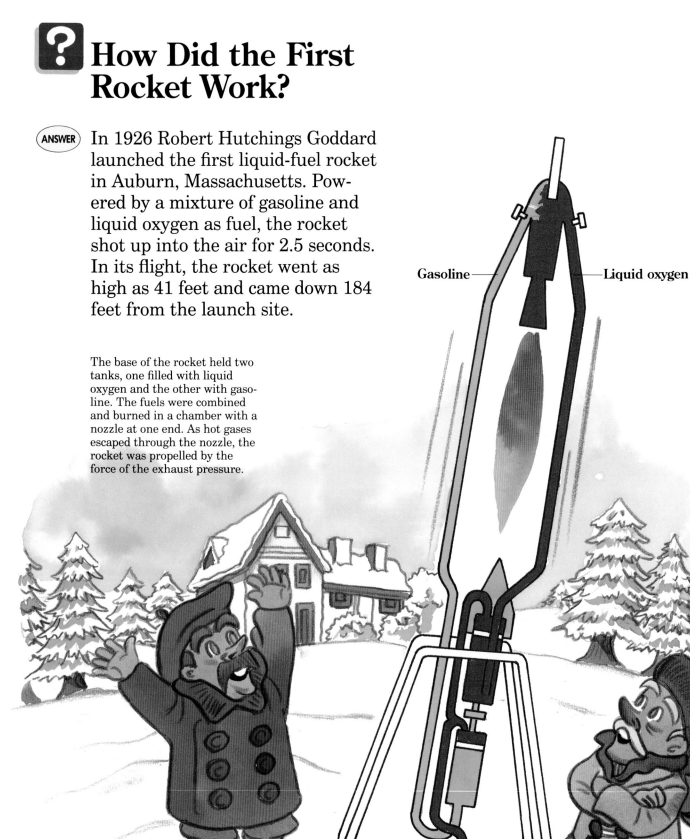

Gasoline

Liquid oxygen

■ The role of gunpowder

In the 9th century, before anyone thought of traveling into space, the Chinese invented gunpowder. They used gunpowder to make weapons and to shoot the first rocketlike projectiles into the air.

 # What powers modern rockets?

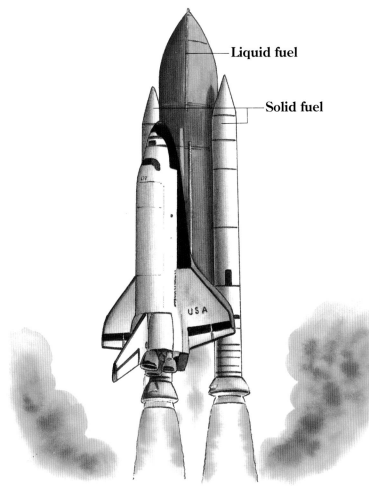

- Liquid fuel

- Solid fuel

The space shuttle is propelled by two solid rocket boosters and three main engines. The solid rocket fuel consists of chemicals similar to the gunpowder of ancient Chinese rockets. The main engines burn a mixture of liquid fuels of the kind used by Goddard.

● To the Parent

In 1903, Konstantin Tsiolkovsky, a Russian mathematician, proposed many of the early theories of astronautics. He envisioned the possibilities of man-made satellites, liquid propellants, spaceships, and spacewalks. The American Robert Goddard experimented with similar ideas and launched the first liquid-fuel rocket in 1926. At the outset of World War II, German scientists developed the V-2 rocket, which was used as a weapon. Later the same rocket was adapted in the Apollo program to put a person on the moon.

When Was Money First Used?

ANSWER In ancient times people made everything they needed themselves. At first people lived in small groups. When more people began to live in one area, farmers grew a greater variety of vegetables and fruits. With so many foods available, they began trading one for another. But because some foods are worth more than others, people invented forms of money to make the exchange easier.

How many apples are equal to one fish? It was not easy to make a fair exchange when one food was worth more than the other.

Some of the first forms of money were shells or clay pieces with markings that gave a value for each. People used them to buy things as we do with metal coins and printed money today.

■ First money

The ancient Sumerians, who lived in what is modern-day Iraq, used clay tokens *(below)* as money. The shape of the token indicated a specific item, and the size showed its quantity. The Chinese first paid with cowrie shells. By 600 B.C. they cast metal tools as money, such as the bronze hoe and knife at right.

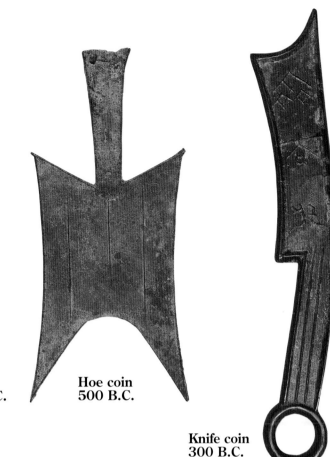

Clay tokens
3000 B.C.

Cowrie shell
7th century B.C.

Hoe coin
500 B.C.

Knife coin
300 B.C.

Early coins

Coins had to be not only strong but lightweight so they would be easy to carry. Metal turned out to be the best material. Gold and silver coins were the most valuable. One of the earliest metal coins is from eastern Turkey *(below left)* and is made of gold and silver. This coin had a simple design; the first minted coins, such as the Croesus gold piece *(below center)* and the Athenian piece *(below right)* showed more complex designs. In many countries coins had holes in them so they could be carried on a string, like the Japanese coin *(near right)*. An American gold piece of $50 was minted in 1852.

Japanese coin
7th century

$50 gold piece
19th century

Lydian coin
700 B.C.

Croesus coin
700 B.C.

Athenian coin
500 B.C.

❓ What Were the First Clocks Like?

(ANSWER) The first people on earth had no need for accurate time. They divided their days by the rising and setting of the sun and counted the years by the seasons. About 3,500 years ago, people began to show the passing of time through clever inventions.

Long ago, people could tell time by the position of the sun in the sky. In ancient Egypt stone monuments like the obelisk below served as sundials that tracked time by the advancing shadow.

A Greek water clock

■ Clocks that burned time away

◄ A candle clock was simply a candle marked with the hours of the day. Each colored segment lasted for about an hour. The number where the burning stopped showed what time it was.

◄ Some clocks burned oil to measure the passing of time. People could read off the hour of the day by the level of oil left in the lamp.

■ Watches and clocks

In the first watches a coiled metal spring moved a single hand as the spring unwound. A pendulum clock was turned by a drum, which was pulled by weights. The drum's motion was transmitted to an escape wheel. The teeth of the escape wheel were caught by a bar at the top of the pendulum rod.

A watch run by a windup spring ◄

A clock advanced ▶ by a pendulum

● **To the Parent**

The first mechanical clocks, driven by hanging weights, were bulky and heavy. They hung mainly in churches and public buildings. Clocks became popular in homes in the 17th century, when the invention of the coiled-spring and pendulum types allowed for building smaller models. Louis Cartier created the first wrist watch for aviator Alberto Santos-Dumont in 1907.

How Did People Come Up with a Calendar?

The first people measured the year by the seasons. They followed the cycles of the sun and the moon but ended up with years that were too long or too short. Today's calendar began in 1582 when Pope Gregory XIII's astronomers chose a year of 365 days and a leap year every four years.

■ Moon calendar

The Babylonians were the first people to use a calendar, about 5,000 years ago. They measured a year by observing the phases of the moon. But a moon calendar is not exact. It has only 354 days instead of 365 days in a year.

◼ Sun calendar

At first the ancient Egyptians based their calendars on the phases of the moon. When they observed the position of the sun as the earth turned around it, however, they noticed that the year was longer than the moon cycle, so they switched to a sun calendar instead.

◼ Pope Gregory's conference

◼ Julian calendar

The Roman general Julius Caesar copied the Egyptians but added days at the end of the year to make it 365 days long. This calendar, called the Julian calendar, was adopted in 46 B.C.; it lasted until the Gregorian calendar was introduced.

When Did People Start Eating with Spoons and Forks?

ANSWER In ancient times people ate with their fingers. For soup or stew they used shells or pieces of wood. They cut their food with sharpened stones until they knew how to make metal blades. Soon thereafter people started eating with their knives. About 1,000 years ago they began shaping metal into forks. Little by little they changed the number of prongs to make the tools into the forks we use today.

■ Spoons

At first people ate with shells or wood hollowed out at one end and shaped like spoons.

■ Forks

Before the invention of forks, people speared their food with the points of their knives.

❓ What about chopsticks?

Chopsticks are much older than forks. People in China ate with them as long as 5,000 years ago. Some ancient chopsticks were joined at one end like tweezers. *Chop* comes from the Chinese word *kuai-zi,* meaning "quick."

The fork was invented when people wanted a better tool for eating than the knife. The shape of forks changed slowly from something to spear food with to the curved form with four prongs we know today. This shape serves best for scooping up most foods.

● To the Parent

Shells and sticks shaped into wooden spoons were probably the first eating utensils. Forks appeared in Italy about A.D. 1100. Curiously enough, they were said to be used only for eating berries and other foods likely to stain the diner's fingers. When Catherine de Médicis married King Henry II in 1533, she brought forks and Italian table manners to the French court. The exact origin of chopsticks is unknown, but they may have begun in China and spread from there to Korea, Japan, and other Asian countries.

Why Do We Use Toothpaste?

ANSWER Long before toothpaste was invented, people cleaned their teeth to keep them white and free of food particles. At first only kings and wealthy people used a powder that they mixed with water to form a paste. The ingredients often included powdered deer antlers and powdered cattle hoofs.

■ Toothpaste ingredients

Herbs

Powdered deer antlers

Honey

Powdered cattle hoofs and bones

■ Fauchard's toothpaste

Soap and lime were combined to make a paste.

Coral and sea-shells were ground into a scouring powder.

An extract from the bark of the soapwort tree was mixed with water.

Pierre Fauchard, an 18th-century French dentist, developed the first toothpaste that was similar to what we use today. Fauchard dipped a sponge in warm water and used a mixture of the ingredients shown above to clean his teeth.

Where did toothbrushes come from?

A long time ago people didn't use toothbrushes. They rinsed their mouths with water and rubbed their fingers across their teeth. In some countries people chewed on sticks until the ends became bristly like a brush and polished their teeth with the bristles. They also sharpened sticks to a point to clean between their teeth, which is how we use toothpicks today.

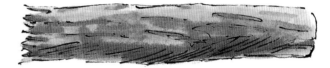

▲ **Chew stick**

▲ **Toothpick**

Toothbrushes were first used by persons of high rank in China. In time the custom spread from there to Europe.

● **To the Parent**

The earliest evidence of tooth powder was found in ancient Egypt, where it was used for cosmetic and hygienic purposes. People made it into a paste, spread it on a finger, and rubbed it on the teeth. By 1498 the Chinese were making bristle toothbrushes. Only since the 18th century, when people began to understand the causes of tooth decay, have they developed powders and pastes to keep teeth and gums healthy.

When Was Soap Used for the First Time?

ANSWER Before anyone thought of making soap, people used a mixture of wood ashes and water to loosen the dirt in clothes. Many years later someone decided to bind the powdery ashes with animal fat to make a solid cake. And that was the first bar of soap.

▲ The first soap we know about was made by the ancient Phoenicians on the Mediterranean coast of what is modern-day Lebanon. They boiled a mixture of goat fat and wood ashes in water until a scum formed on the surface. When the scum became thick, they scooped it up and let it dry into soap.

■ The first soap

Mediterranean Sea

■ Early detergents

Before soap was known, people washed with plant juices that made a lot of lather. They boiled the bark or berries of the soapwort tree and used the liquid the same way we use detergent. Before washing machines existed, they washed clothes by hand in rivers, by stamping on them with their feet, by rubbing them against stones, or by beating them with a stick.

▲ Soapberries

Olive trees

Italy

Because the first soaps were made with animal fat, they smelled bad. People living in the countries around the Mediterranean used olive oil instead of animal fat and made soap that had a pleasant smell.

MINI-DATA

The word for soap sounds similar in many languages. *Shabon*, the old Japanese word for soap, is said to have come from *saboten*, for cactus, because the juice of the cactus was used like soap. *Sekken* is used today in Japan. But it also sounds like the French *savon* and the Portuguese *savão*. The German word *Seife* for soap is said to come from the Latin *sebum* for tallow.

● **To the Parent**

Soap is probably an invention of the ancient Phoenicians, who combined wood ashes and water. Later they mixed the ashes with animal fats and derived a formula of five parts of potassium carbonate made from wood ashes, such as beech, mixed with one part of fat. The animal fats often made the soap smell rancid. The mixture was also caustic and not suitable for washing the body. Regular production of soap began in the 8th century when the unpleasant odor could be overcome. People began mixing olive oil with the ash of seaweed to create pleasantly scented soaps.

What Made People Think of Glasses?

ANSWER Before eyeglasses were invented, people used crystals and precious stones as magnifying glasses. Eyeglasses as we know them today appeared in Italy during the 13th century. When glassblowers handled curved glass of different thicknesses, they noticed that the glass seemed to bring objects closer. With that idea in mind, they shaped glass into lenses and held them together with wire.

△ Crystal magnifying lenses have been in use since ancient times.

■ Italian glassmaking

Glass begins as a mixture of sand, soda, and limestone that is melted. Glassmakers blow the hot liquid mixture, like soap bubbles, through a thin tube. While experimenting with glass, they discovered that it could magnify objects.

△ The first glasses simply rested on a person's nose.

■ Types of glasses

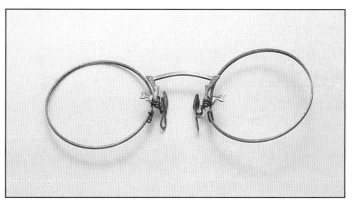

▲ The pince-nez, meaning "pinch the nose" in French, clamped onto the bridge of the nose with a spring device.

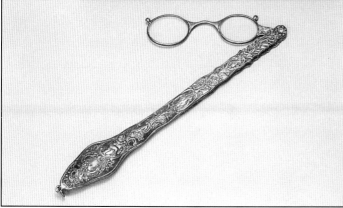

▲ A lorgnette was a fancifully ornamented pair of glasses with a long handle that served to hold them to the eyes.

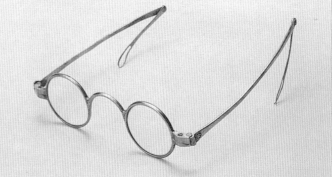

▲ The first glasses with sidepieces to fit over the ears were made in England in the 18th century.

● To the Parent

The oldest lens in existence, dating from about 700 B.C., was found in ruins in Assyria. The lens was a polished crystal that served to magnify the rays of the sun to start a fire. Eyeglasses were invented by a physicist in Italy in the 13th century. The glassmakers of Murano near Venice produced the first glasses and kept the art a secret.

❓ Who Developed Sneakers?

(ANSWER) In cold-weather countries people wrapped their feet in animal skins before they had shoes. In warmer climates they did not need shoes. But in South America, Indians protected the soles of their feet by dipping them in latex, the tree sap from which rubber is made. This use led to the idea of rubber-soled canvas shoes.

■ How Goodyear improved rubber

In the 1830s Charles Goodyear was trying to make rubber more flexible and durable. In his research he accidentally dropped a rubber-sulfur mixture on a hot stove. When the material cooled, Goodyear had discovered vulcanization—a process that makes rubber resistant to cracking. Among the products made possible by this discovery were the shoes we call sneakers.

■ Shoes from around the world

People have been wearing shoes for thousands of years, and styles have been as different as the customs in each country. In ancient times, people in Egypt wore sandals made of leather or braided fibers. In Rome, senators wore sandals with four black leather straps wound around their calves as a symbol of rank. For hundreds of years in Russia, heavy felt boots kept feet warm. The styles varied depending on climate and the purpose of the shoe.

▲ In India, slippers are made of cloth and have toes that curl back.

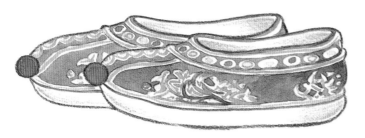

▲ Cloth shoes from China are slightly raised at the toes.

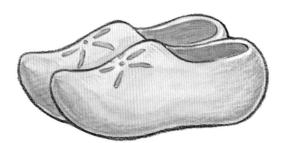

▲ Wooden shoes worn in Holland serve to keep the feet dry in wet and soggy soil.

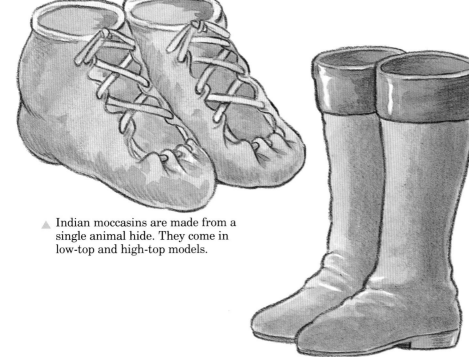

▲ Indian moccasins are made from a single animal hide. They come in low-top and high-top models.

▲ People wear boots in most cold-weather countries.

● **To the Parent**

The first shoes in Egypt were sandals made from woven papyrus strips, worn only by members of the upper class. The Greeks made leather sandals; the Moors sewed shoes of rope and hemp; and people in cold climates wrapped furs or animal skins around their feet. For thousands of years shoemakers sewed shoes by hand. In the 19th century, after the invention of the sewing machine, shoemakers began to use lasts for shaping shoes and sewing them by machine, marking the beginning of mass production.

? When Did People Begin to Use Umbrellas?

ANSWER Umbrellas were used in China as long as 3,000 years ago by the emperor and other high-ranking people of the court. An umbrella indicated a person's rank rather than serving as protection from the rain. In ancient Greece women carried parasols—sun umbrellas—to guard against the sun.

■ A man's umbrella

In 18th-century Europe, women made the parasol fashionable again as a sunshade. Men thought that was silly. But Jonas Hanway of England began to use an umbrella to shield himself from the rain. He had the habit of taking an umbrella with him whether it rained or not. At first people laughed at him; eventually they decided it made sense to keep dry, and British gentlemen began carrying umbrellas, calling them "Hanways."

■ Uses for umbrellas

▲ In ancient China, people of high rank had servants to carry their umbrellas. Besides the umbrella, the servants held signs decorated with symbols that indicated their leader's status.

▲ In ancient Greece, women screened out the hot rays of the sun with parasols. The name *parasol* means "guard against the sun."

？ How people kept dry

Before people had umbrellas, they kept dry in rainy weather by wearing tightly woven capes or water-repellent cloaks and hats made by weaving waxy leaves and grass together.

● To the Parent

The first umbrellas in China were made with frames of wisteria or sandalwood, covered with leaves or feathers. These mainly symbolized a person's rank. Early Egyptians stretched papyrus over the frame. For a long time umbrellas served only to protect a person from too much sun. In 1750 Englishman Jonas Hanway used an umbrella for the first time in the rain. Others laughed, but it was a sensible idea. At first it was not considered good manners for a man to use an umbrella, and soldiers were forbidden to use them at all. But eventually umbrellas came into fashion. By the 1840s Henry Holland had devised steel ribs for umbrellas, leading to mass production of umbrellas. The folding umbrella was invented in Germany in 1930.

Who Were the First People to Look into Mirrors?

ANSWER Water was the first mirror. People saw their faces reflected in ponds and rivers. Another early mirror was a shiny black stone called obsidian. But neither stones nor water gave a clear reflection. When people learned how to polish metal to a shiny surface, they used bronze mirrors. Mirrors today are made of glass coated with silver.

■ Mirrors made of obsidian

Obsidian, a volcanic stone that is similar to black glass, was used in early times as a mirror.

◀ **Obsidian**

▲ An Asian mirror   ▲ A European mirror

■ Bronze mirrors

Bronze is a metal made of a mixture of tin and copper, developed by early civilizations. Metalworkers found that if they made a flat piece of bronze and polished it well, it could serve as a crude mirror.

■ The first mirrors

In 1508 the glassmakers of Venice invented a mirror made of glass. They coated the backside of a sheet of glass with tin and mercury, which made it shiny and reflected images perfectly.

● **To the Parent**

Water has been used as a mirror since time immemorial. Hand-held mirrors, like those of obsidian or bronze, were precious items. The mercury-tin coated mirror was so revolutionary in terms of simplicity and cost that the technique was a closely guarded secret. By 1840 the tin-mercury mixture was replaced with a silver coating, which is still in use today. The invention of rolled plate glass in the 17th century permitted the making of full-length mirrors.

How Were Hula Hoops, Frisbees, and Yo-Yos Invented?

ANSWER Children often think up their own toys and games. Hula Hoops probably were the same hoops children used to push along on the street with sticks as long as 3,000 years ago. It is possible that those children spun the hoops around their waists when they got tired of chasing them.

■ The first hoop

■ Frisbee launch

Frisbees, the plastic disks you throw through the air, were invented when college students amused themselves by throwing empty pie tins at one another.

■ The original yo-yo

An early Chinese toy consisted of two ivory disks spun on a silk cord. In the 16th century, Philippine hunters used a similar object as a weapon and called it a yo-yo.

● To the Parent

Hula Hoops were all the rage in the 1950s, but the fad ended when doctors found that spinning the hoop caused back and neck injuries. Frisbee is a slightly different spelling of the name stamped on the pie tins of the Frisbie Pie Company of Bridgeport, Connecticut. Three American universities—Harvard, Princeton, and Yale—claim to have originated the game in the 1940s, when students started throwing the empty tins at one another. The yo-yo, which was once used as a weapon in Southeast Asia, was brought to France by French missionaries.

Who Made the First Jigsaw Puzzle?

ANSWER In 1760 John Spilsbury, a young map-maker and printer in England, made a game out of teaching geography. He mounted engraved maps on sheets of mahogany and cut them apart along country and county lines with a jigsaw. By putting the pieces back in place, children learned about countries of the world. This idea led to puzzles on different subjects with interlocking pieces. Today puzzles may consist of as many as 5,000 pieces.

■ An array of puzzles

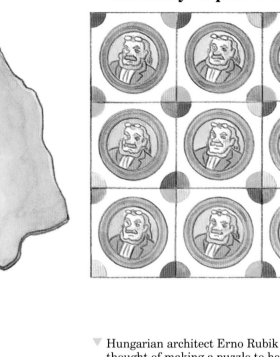

The object of this puzzle is to arrange the nine pictures into a single square, without using the same color twice in any of the ball sections.

When the sliding block puzzle is scrambled, the player has to arrange the numbers in sequence by moving them through the empty space.

Hungarian architect Erno Rubik thought of making a puzzle to help his students understand the idea of three dimensions. He developed a puzzle known as Rubik's Cube, then took more than a month to solve it himself.

? What Did the First Bicycle Look Like?

ANSWER The first bicycle, built in 1818, had wooden wheels without pedals. Riders pushed the bicycles with their feet on the ground. Inventors soon made bicycles easier to ride by adding pedals, chains, brakes, and rubber tires.

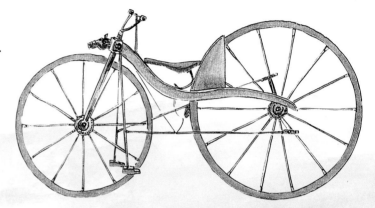

▲ A Scottish blacksmith named Kirkpatrick Macmillan first thought of adding pedals to the bicycle, which was then called a hobbyhorse. He installed the pedals below the handlebars and connected them with long rods to the rear-wheel axle. The pedals—called treadles—worked with an up-and-down motion.

◄ In France, Pierre Michaux and his son Ernest built the velocipede, a bicycle with a large wheel in front and a smaller one in back. The bike had pedals at the front wheel and iron rims around the wooden wheels.

The penny-farthing bicycle could go faster than the velocipede because its front wheel was much larger than its rear wheel. One turn of the pedals propelled the penny-farthing a great distance. The seat sat above the front wheel to make pedaling easier.

About 100 years ago bicycles began to look more modern. Called safety bicycles, they had wheels of equal size, rubber tires, and a chain drive. Today, bikes are built for racing, mountain biking, popping wheelies, and just-plain-fun riding.

● To the Parent

In 1818, German Baron Karl von Drais exhibited the first bicycle in Paris. Riders propelled this two-wheeled machine by pushing their feet against the ground. Twenty years later Kirkpatrick Macmillan, a Scottish blacksmith, improved the bicycle by equipping it with pedals that hung from the handlebars. The next generation of bicycles came with pedals connected to the front wheel. The penny-farthing, named for its large front wheel, which resembled the British penny, and its small back wheel, which looked like the farthing—a coin one-fourth the value of the penny—could move faster than other bicycles. In 1889, John Dunlop, a Belfast veterinarian, introduced a pneumatic tire. The new tire, together with rear-wheel gear-and-chain arrangements, made bicycles a popular form of transportation.

Have Fireworks Been Around for a Long Time?

ANSWER Nearly 2,000 years ago the Chinese invented fireworks. They stuffed a tube of bamboo with charcoal, sulfur, and saltpeter, ignited the mixture, and threw it into the air. This novelty spread from China to the Middle East and from there to Europe. At first fireworks were no more than flying firecrackers that made a lot of noise and smoke. About 600 years ago the Italians learned how to make the explosions last longer. In the 19th century they added chemicals that gave off flashes of yellow and orange.

■ Italian fireworks

■ Chinese fireworks

The first fireworks, set off during festivals in China, made a lot of noise. The Chinese exploded them in hopes of scaring away evil spirits.

■ Modern fireworks

Today, fireworks come in glorious colors, flashing from yellow and red to green and blue, with surprising star- and flower-shaped bursts.

● **To the Parent**

Fireworks began when a Chinese cook combined sulfur, saltpeter, and charcoal in the kitchen—or so the story goes—and the mixture accidentally exploded. Before long the Chinese found good use for these explosives. They packed the ingredients into tubes of bamboo and sent the tubes flying into the air. The tubes burst in noisy explosions and became a daytime entertainment to ward off evil spirits at weddings and to celebrate victories or the New Year. Not until the latter half of the 14th century did fireworks light up the night sky in Florence, Italy.

How Did We Get Pencils?

ANSWER

Ever since the discovery of graphite, a soft, coal-like substance, people have tried to write with it. But graphite loses its shape with use. So people wrapped it in string or tried to support it with braces, making the earliest pencils.

▲ One of the first pencils looked like the picture above. It consisted of a piece of graphite held between two pieces of wood that were tied together with string.

Although graphite worked well for writing, it came apart easily and smeared in the writer's hands.

▼ Inventors mixed many different materials with graphite, trying to make the substance harder. N. J. Conté came up with what we use as pencil lead today: a mixture of graphite, sulfur, and clay.

■ Grades of hardness

Manufacturers list degrees of hardness for the lead of pencils, indicated by letters from B for soft to H for hard, or by numbers ranging from No. 1, the softest, through the common No. 2, a medium-soft pencil, to the hardest—No. 4.

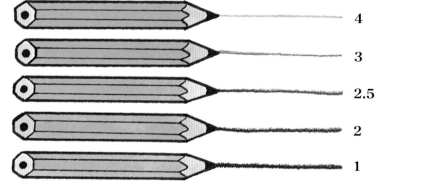

4

3

2.5

2

1

■ Antique pen

For 1,000 years people wrote with quills, the feathers from the tail or wing of a goose. The quill was sharpened at the tip and dipped in ink.

■ Modern pens

American Lewis Edson Waterman invented the first successful fountain pen in 1884. The ballpoint pen came much later; it was developed by Hungarians Lazlo and Georg Biro in 1935.

 Who Built the First Roller Skates?

ANSWER The first skates were ice skates, invented in countries where rivers stayed frozen for a long time in winter. Belgium was such a country. A Belgian named Joseph Merlin tried to skate on smooth floors by substituting wheels for the skates' blades. In 1759 he appeared at a masked ball in London on rolling skates, playing his violin. But his homemade skates did not work well. When he tried to stop, he crashed into a mirror.

■ Early roller skates

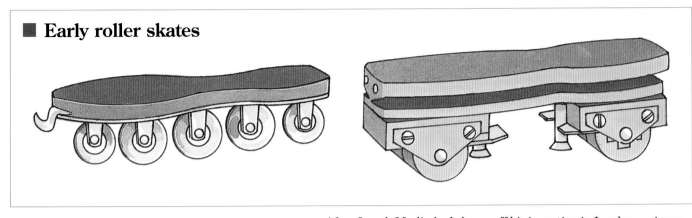

I wish I could skate in summer too.

▲ After Joseph Merlin had shown off his invention in London, a singer appeared on roller skates in an ice-skating scene of an opera in Paris. Since people did not know how to make an indoor ice-skating rink, they rolled in on skates like the one shown at top left. The first roller skate that let the wearer spin around and stop is shown at right.

■ Modern skates

Using today's models, roller skaters can spin and twirl and compete in high-speed races. In-line skates, often called Roller-blades, with their wheels arranged in a single row, gave rise to roller hockey games.

● To the Parent

Joseph Merlin of Belgium invented roller skates in 1759. He made a dramatic entry at a masked ball in London, skating on wheeled shoes and playing his violin. His construction was crude, and he had no way of controlling the rollers. When he tried to come to a stop, he crashed into a mirror and was seriously injured. Various inventors made improvements. But skates did not become popular until 1884, when ball-bearing wheels were introduced. With in-line skates, a skater can go as fast as 45 miles per hour.

Why Were Zippers Invented?

ANSWER Until 1893 people could fasten their clothes and shoes only with buttons and laces. Whitcomb L. Judson of the United States thought he could come up with something better. He invented a gadget he called a clasp locker, made of tiny hooks and eyes. But this zipper kept coming undone. A Swedish engineer named Gideon Sundback improved on Judson's invention and made the first zipper with gripping metal teeth.

▲ **Zippered galoshes**

■ Shoelace blues

People got tired of tying the laces on old-fashioned high-top shoes and boots. With a zipper they could quickly fasten rubber boots, which stayed well sealed in rainy weather.

■ First zippers

Shortly after the invention of the zipper, during World War I, the U.S. Army and Navy tested the new fastener. They found they needed less fabric for uniforms that zipped instead of buttoned and began to sew zippers into pilots' flight suits.

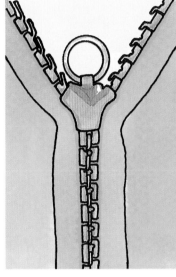
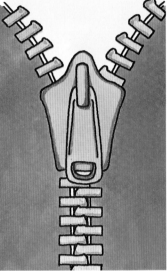

▲ Zipper from 1906   ▲ Today's zipper

 ## Why do we call it zipper?

Salespeople were looking for a name that would describe how the fastener zipped along as it was being closed. Suddenly they knew and named it the zipper.

●To the Parent

A zipperlike fastener was invented in 1893 when Whitcomb L. Judson of Chicago took out a patent for a fastener as an alternative to buttons and laces. In 1906 a Swedish engineer named Gideon Sundback, who worked for Judson, created a metal zipper with interlocking teeth. He patented his invention in 1913. Before long the B. F. Goodrich Company marketed galoshes fastened with the new gadget and may have come up with the name, calling it the zipper shoe. Another story has it that a salesman demonstrating the zipper shouted, "Zip! It's open! Zip! It's closed!" and the name stuck.

Where Did the Idea for Velcro Come From?

ANSWER

In 1948 Georges de Mestral of Switzerland was hiking in the Alps. After a day's hike, he found cockleburs clinging to his trousers and socks, and he had a hard time taking them off. He looked at the burs closely and noticed that they had tiny hooks on the end that stuck to loops in the fabric of his clothing. These burs gave him the idea to make similar hooks and loops for fastening clothes. He asked a French weaver to help him develop this fastener, and after eight years they came up with Velcro.

Some plant seeds like the cockle-bur have tiny hooks that catch in the fur of animals passing by. This is nature's way of carrying seeds to other areas.

■ **Nature's fasteners**

■ How Velcro works

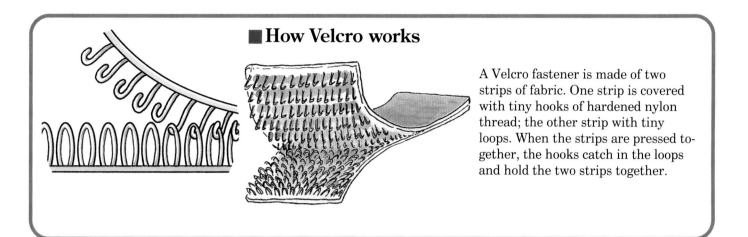

A Velcro fastener is made of two strips of fabric. One strip is covered with tiny hooks of hardened nylon thread; the other strip with tiny loops. When the strips are pressed together, the hooks catch in the loops and hold the two strips together.

❓ Uses for Velcro

Shoes

Spacesuits

Bags

Velcro is an easy fastener for the objects shown on this page and is used for many others as well. The inventor hoped that Velcro would replace the zipper. Although Velcro has not done that, there are uses for both inventions.

●To the Parent

Georges de Mestral of Switzerland invented Velcro—named for velvet and crochet hook—in 1948, just when zippers had become popular. Textile manufacturers showed little interest in a new fastener then. Instead of giving up, de Mestral began working with a weaver in Lyon, France, to produce a strip of cotton with hooks and eyes. By the mid-1950s, when a process was found to harden nylon thread, de Mestral changed to nylon tape, which proved sturdy and locked solidly.

How Did Blue Jeans Become Popular?

(ANSWER) In the 1850s, when the California gold rush was at its height, a young tailor named Levi Strauss from Bavaria, Germany, traveled west to try his luck. Panning for gold was tough work, and goldminers tore their clothes every day. Instead of looking for gold, Levi Strauss decided to sew trousers from strong canvas from the Italian city of Genoa, called Gênes in French, or "jeans" in a rough pronunciation of the word. The trousers were so sturdy, everybody wanted a pair.

■ Tough jeans

■ The first jeans

Levi Strauss sewed the first jeans from the same white material that he used to make tents and wagon covers. Although these trousers were very strong, they were not perfect for the job because they quickly got dirty in the mines.

Why are jeans blue?

To make the white jeans more practical, Levi Strauss dyed the fabric with the most popular dye of the time, the juice of the indigo plant. Indigo makes a bright blue color that stays in the fabric permanently.

▲ Juice from the leaves and stalks of the indigo plant is used as a blue dye.

● To the Parent

After his success with canvas trousers, Levi Strauss replaced the tough fabric with a slightly softer material. The fabric became known as denim, because it was sold as *serge de Nîmes*, from the French city of that name. Although the fabric was strong, the miners still complained that the pockets tore easily from holding heavy tools. That's when the tailor strengthened the pockets with copper rivets.

Who Thought Up Soccer, Baseball, and Basketball?

ANSWER A kickball game similar to soccer has been played in England for centuries. Although people enjoyed the game, the players often got into noisy scuffles, injuring many team members. About 100 years ago English clubs had a meeting to set new rules and make the game safer. From then on they called it soccer. Baseball probably came from the English game called cricket. Basketball was invented by James Naismith at the International YMCA College in Springfield, Massachusetts, in 1891.

■ **Early soccer game**

■ Cricket

In cricket a batsman defends a wicket from the ball. If the batsman hits the ball and trades places with another batsman, he scores a run. A team is at bat until 10 players are out.

Cricket, England's national game, was brought to the U.S. by the first settlers. The game is played with a bat and ball by two teams of 11 players. People gradually changed the rules of the game and called it baseball. In 1845 Alexander Cartwright began the first baseball club—the Knickerbocker Club of New York—and created new rules.

■ Basketball

Basketball was conceived by an American professor as a game that could be played indoors in winter. The school's janitor installed half-bushel peach baskets on poles, and the team played with a soccer ball.

● **To the Parent**

Sports like soccer, in which many players kick a ball around, have been popular since ancient times. In England teams from different towns played the game by different rules. In 1863 English soccer clubs met in London to set up common rules. They also banned the use of hands, distinguishing soccer from rugby. The first baseball team was formed in the United States in 1845, and the game soon became a national pastime. Basketball was thought up by James Naismith at the request of Luther Gulick, head of the physical education department of the International YMCA College. Naismith provided written rules, including the size of the ball and the number of players on a team.

Who Made the First Sandwich?

More than 200 years ago an English lord was so fond of card games that he did not even want to take time out to eat. He ordered his servant to put sliced meat and cheese between two pieces of bread so he could eat with one hand and continue to play with the other. The lord was the fourth earl of Sandwich, and sandwiches are named for him.

■ A sandwich gallery

In other countries bread and sandwich fillings are different. In France the filling may be ham and cheese; in Germany, a sausage; in the United States, peanut butter and jelly or cheese and meat with lettuce and tomatoes.

Sausage

Germany

Ham and cheese

France

Cheese with lettuce and tomato

United States

? What about hamburgers?

In the German city of Hamburg, tough meat was often pounded and shredded to make it tender. Immigrants brought this recipe to the U.S. They fried the shredded meat and served it between two slices of bread, calling it the Hamburg steak.

● To the Parent

Britain's John Montagu, the fourth earl of Sandwich and first lord of the admiralty, was a compulsive gambler. At times he refused to leave the card table to eat a proper meal. In 1762 he was said to have instructed his butler to put meat and cheese between slices of buttered bread so he could eat without interrupting his game. Although meat and bread combinations had been eaten elsewhere before, the story struck people's fancy, and they began calling the combination a sandwich.

❓ Who Ate the First Ice Cream?

ANSWER The first version of ice cream was served to the emperor of China 4,000 years ago. His cooks prepared a dessert made from fruit and juice and packed it in snow to chill. Some 2,000 years later, the Romans had the same idea, when the emperor Nero had ice carried down from the mountains to chill fruit.

■ A treat from Naples

By the 19th century ice cream could be bought in stores all over the world. Procopio Cultelli of Italy introduced Neapolitan-style ice cream, consisting of vanilla-, strawberry-, and chocolate-flavored ices, in his shop in Paris.

■ Making ice cream

Cream, sugar, and flavorings are mixed in a small container, which sits in a larger container filled with ice and salt.

The inside container is turned until the mixture freezes.

■ Frozen fruit

The Roman emperor Nero had his cooks pack fruit and ice into boxes. The fruit became half-frozen and could be eaten the way we eat sherbet.

■ Fruit ices in China

In 13th-century China, street vendors sold fruit-flavored ices from pushcarts.

How Did We Get Frozen Food?

ANSWER Clarence Birdseye, an American fur trader, was traveling through Labrador in winter when he saw fishermen catching fish that froze as soon as they came out of the water. He learned that the frozen fish would still be good to eat months later. Birdseye wondered if other foods could be preserved by freezing and began to experiment.

■ How food is frozen

Boxes of fresh food are stacked between
tubes filled with a coolant. As the coolant
runs through the tubes, it absorbs heat
from the food.

▲ A frozen-food warehouse

67

? Who Produced Plastic and Materials like It?

ANSWER Plastic can't be found in nature like cotton or stone. Englishman Alexander Parkes invented the first man-made material in the 1850s by mixing chemicals with plant matter, pressing them into a mold, and heating them. This process resulted in a hard but flexible substance, which he named Parkesine.

■ **Ivory substitute**

The American John W. Hyatt improved on Parkes's invention and called the substance celluloid. He was trying to concoct a substitute for ivory from which billiard balls could be made. Although they looked like ivory, the celluloid balls exploded easily when they bumped into one another, and they sometimes caught fire. But celluloid worked well as a material for film and shirt-collar stiffeners.

■ Bakelite

The first all man-made material was Bakelite, invented by Leo Baekeland, a Belgian-American chemist. By heating chemicals from coal, petroleum, and natural gas, he made a material useful for telephones and light-bulb insulation.

■ Nylon

Nylon is a fiber spun from plastic and used in many different fabrics. When nylon was first invented, people were excited about the new thread because it looked and felt like silk.

Many things are made of plastic. What can you think of that is made of this miracle substance?

●To the Parent

Plastic is a man-made material that can be shaped easily when heated. British chemist Alexander Parkes developed the first plastic material, a mixture of nitrocellulose softened by vegetable oils and camphor, which he named Parkesine. John W. Hyatt of the United States recognized the valuable qualities of the new material and began to improve it, calling his mixture celluloid. Bakelite, invented by Leo Baekeland, was the first completely synthetic plastic. Because it withstood heat and did not conduct electricity, it was used to insulate electrical equipment and small kitchen appliances.

? When Was the Camera Invented?

ANSWER A box that projected images onto a wall was called a camera in the 16th century, but film did not exist. About 300 years later Frenchmen Joseph-Nicéphore Niepce and Louis Daguerre took pictures using metal plates. In 1888 George Eastman invented a way to take pictures with the box camera and film.

■ Daguerre's camera

In 1839 Daguerre made a camera of two wooden boxes, one sliding inside the other. A lens on the outer box could be moved in and out of a tube to focus on an object. Instead of using film, he placed a copper plate coated with silver at the back of the camera. It took him 30 minutes to take a photograph. This worked only for landscapes and motionless objects. People couldn't hold still that long to have their pictures taken.

▲ An early Daguerre photograph

■ An artist's camera

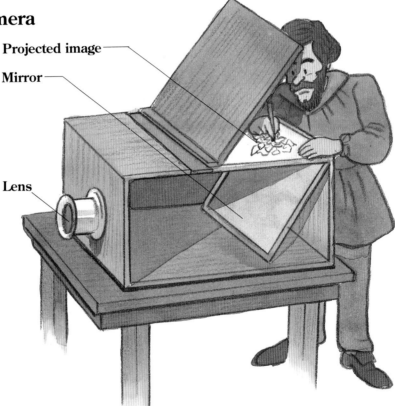

Projected image

Mirror

Lens

The first cameras were tracing tools. The image of an object, like the vase at left, was projected through the lens to a mirror, which cast the image onto a screen on top.

● To the Parent

In the 16th century an Italian scientist invented the *camera obscura*, meaning "dark room," which projected an outside image onto the back wall of a room. A smaller, boxlike camera obscura was a tracing tool for artists. In the 1830s Joseph-Nicéphore Niepce, a French physicist, experimented with preserving the projected image by applying photosensitive asphalt to the back wall of the box. Louis Daguerre improved the sensitivity of the chemicals and began making daguerreotypes.

? How Did Television Begin?

ANSWER Television was developed through the combined efforts of many people. Some inventors figured out how to transmit images, and others thought up a method for having the images show on the television screen. The most important contributions were made by three men: Karl Ferdinand Braun of Germany, John L. Baird of Britain, and Vladimir K. Zworykin of the United States.

■ Inventors of television

▲ **Karl Braun's tube**

German physicist Karl Braun invented a method of moving streams of electrons by converting electrical pulses into light and dark areas. As the glass tube lit up, pictures formed on its back wall.

▼ Baird's televisor

British scientist John L. Baird built the televisor. His machine could split a picture into a number of lines. This process, called scanning, is still used in TV transmissions today.

● To the Parent

Experiments with TV began in 1897 with Karl Braun's invention of the cathode-ray tube. Zworykin improved on Baird's mechanical scanning by scanning images electronically, which divided a picture into tiny picture elements later called pixels. A camera projected these pixels as electrical impulses onto a picture tube to re-create the image at a rate of 30 pictures per second.

Vladimir Zworykin made a camera called an iconoscope *(below)*, which divided a picture into dots. The dots were sent by electricity and converted into an image on the TV screen.

◄ Iconoscope

? Were There Early Calculators?

(ANSWER) In the distant past people used their fingers or pebbles to make calculations. But they soon needed help. The first calculator was the abacus, which is still used today in some countries. It consists of a wooden frame with beads on rods. Centuries after the invention of the abacus, mechanical calculating machines came into use, followed by modern ones powered by electricity.

■ Different calculators

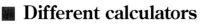

The Chinese abacus was one of the first calculators. It has two beads on the rods in the upper section, which count as five each. Five beads on the rods of the lower section count as one each.

▶ Before the invention of calculators, people used their fingers to do complex arithmetic.

In 1642 French mathematician Blaise Pascal invented a machine that could add and subtract. The calculator worked by a series of cogs and wheels that could display numbers up to 999,999.

■ Modern calculators

The more calculations a machine could do, the larger it had to be. But modern calculators, like the ones shown at right, run on batteries and microchips, which makes them small and fast. Some calculators are powered by solar batteries; a few calculators give the answer out loud.

Herman Hollerith built a mechanical tabulator. His invention consisted of a machine that punched holes in cards to indicate numbers. A counter would count the holes and display the numbers on dials as a calculator does on windows today.

This early-20th-century hand-cranked calculator could add and subtract and do multiplication and division.

When Was the Computer Introduced?

ANSWER In 1946 scientists at the University of Pennsylvania introduced the first electronic digital computer, called ENIAC (Electronic Numerical Integrator and Computer). The machine operated with thousands of vacuum tubes and was so big it filled an entire room. Many people worked to improve this model and to develop smaller, faster computers. By 1972 the first computer games had components so small they fit into a box.

■ ENIAC

■ The Mark I's many switches

One of the first computers was the Mark I, operating at Harvard University in 1944. The machine was 50 feet long and worked with more than 3,000 electromechanical switches. The Mark I could perform three calculations per second, which seemed very fast at the time. A modern super-computer, however, can do 10 billion calculations per second.

■ Comparing size

A lineup of computers illustrates how they have shrunk in size, from the very large ENIAC at 180 cubes to the desktop computer at one cube. Notebook-size computers are still smaller.

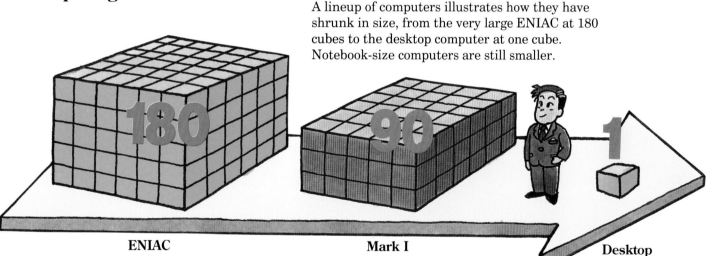

ENIAC   Mark I   Desktop computer

●To the Parent

The first computers were huge because the parts that did calculations consisted of vacuum tubes and mechanical relays. ENIAC used nearly 18,000 vacuum tubes and generated immense heat. The development of microchips, consisting of many thousands of electronic switches and circuits too small to be seen with the naked eye, allowed computers to become smaller. Technology is still moving apace. But some scientists believe a computer with circuits that could duplicate the functioning of the human brain would be much larger than ENIAC.

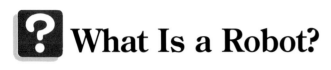

What Is a Robot?

(ANSWER) People often wished for a mechanical helper that could do their work for them. That's where the idea of a robot comes from. The oldest mechanical helper we know of is a Japanese doll. This figure, built in the 17th century, could carry drinks from one place to another. Another early model, made in 1772, was a doll from Switzerland that could draw. Because of these examples we tend to think of robots in human form. But the modern robots used in factories since the 1950s have only hands or eyes.

■ A writing robot

When the robot is wound up like a clock, it dips its quill pen in ink and writes and draws with it.

This mechanical doll built by a Swiss clock-maker is operated by many gears, cogs, and levers that can make it draw or play music.

■ Mechanical servant

This Japanese robot could move forward and backward while serving a drink.

■ Robotic arm

Robots do dangerous work in factories. They also perform jobs that are repeated a lot and that bore people. With sensors, joints, and grippers, a robotic arm, such as the one below, moves faster and more precisely than a human arm.

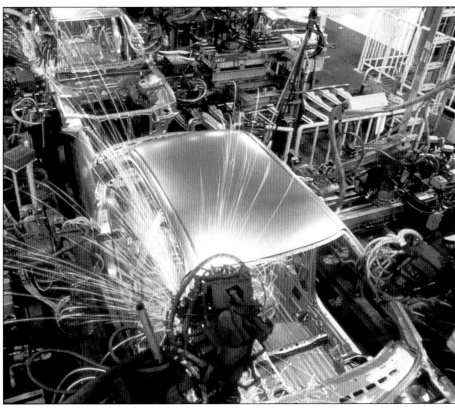

▶ In auto plants robots do much of the work of building cars that people used to do. They can weld and spray-paint hundreds of cars in one day, without getting tired or making a mistake.

● **To the Parent**

Czech playwright Karel Čapek used the term *robot* for machines in human form. The word—from the Czech *robota,* meaning "work"—appeared in his 1920 drama *R.U.R.* (Rossum's Universal Robots). Today robots are used in factories for high-speed jobs requiring precision. Continued research in robotics may yet bring us the cyborgs of science fiction.

? How Did Inventions Help in the House?

■ Cleaning tools

Long ago people swept dirt away with twigs. Later they bound twigs or straw together to make brooms.

▲ Today the electric broom, or vacuum cleaner, helps people pick up dirt.

■ Cooling foods

In ancient times food was kept cool in places like caves. When people learned to move big chunks of ice, they invented the icebox. It was a house or a box filled with blocks of ice that would keep food fresh.

▲ Modern refrigerators chill food through a series of pipes filled with a coolant that lowers the temperature of the air inside.

● To the Parent

Even today, years after the invention of vacuum cleaners and refrigerators, we retain traditional methods of doing things. Many people still use brooms to clean and preserve food the old-fashioned way, by salting or canning.

Growing-Up Album

Which Is the Best Shape to Use?

Here are four pencils and four cups in different shapes. Check one box in each group below to show which object is easiest to use.

■ **Pencils**

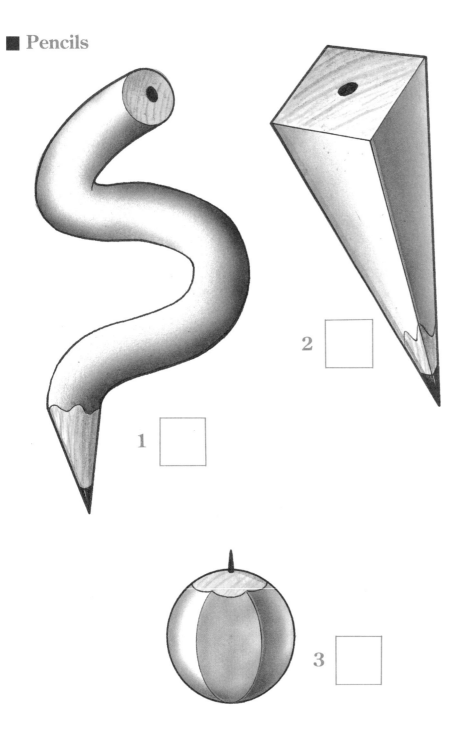

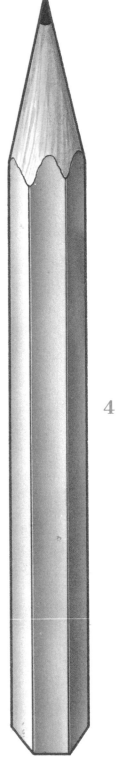

1 ☐

2 ☐

3 ☐

4 ☐

Answer: Pencil No. 4.

■ Cups

Who Invented These?

These drawings show five inventors. What are they famous for? Match each inventor to what he invented.

Printing press

Thomas Edison

Alexander Graham Bell

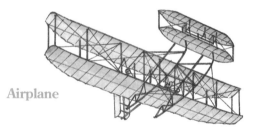

Airplane

Electric light bulb

Orville and Wilbur Wright

Johannes Gutenberg

Telephone

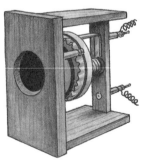

Answers: Edison: Electric light bulb; Bell: Telephone; Wright brothers: Airplane; Gutenberg: Printing press.

How Do You Play with These?

Look at these kids playing. Which part of your body do you use most to play each game? Write one number in each square.

1 Hands   2 Feet/legs   3 Waist

Roller skates

Frisbee

Hula Hoop

Soccer

Yo-yo

Answers: Roller skates: 2; Frisbee: 1; Hula Hoop: 3; Soccer: 2; Yo-yo: 1.

85

Which One Is the Oldest?

Look at the drawings of inventions on these pages. Check one box in each group to show which one you think is the oldest.

Telephones

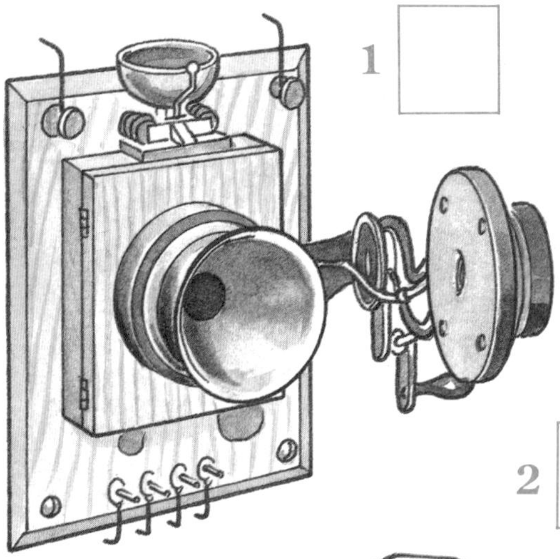

1 ☐

2 ☐

3 ☐

Pencil and pens

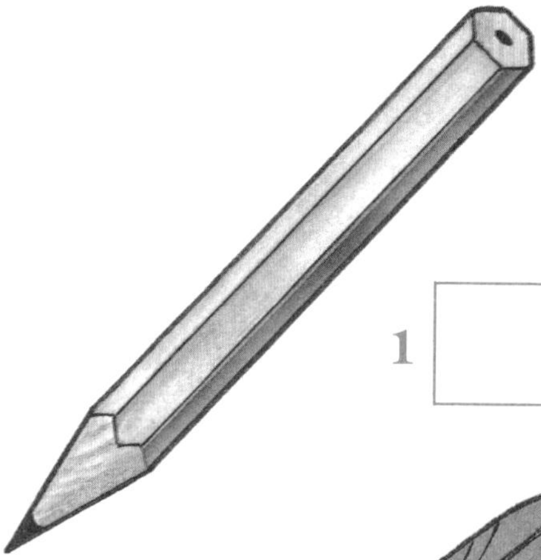

1 ☐

2 ☐

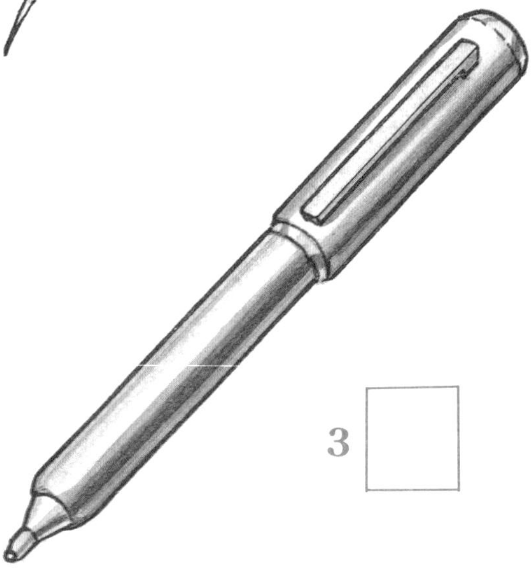

3 ☐

■ Automobiles

1

2

3

■ Airplanes

1

2

3

A Child's First Library of Learning

Staff for
INVENTIONS

Assistant Managing Editor: Patricia Daniels
Editorial Director: Karin Kinney
Research: Marike van der Veen,
    Tamu Sylvia Matrue Turner (intern)
Production Manager: Marlene Zack
Copyeditor: Heidi A. Fritschel
Picture Coordinator: David A. Herod
Production: Celia Beattie
Supervisor of Quality Control: James King
Assistant Supervisor of Quality Control: Miriam Newton
Library: Louise D. Forstall
Computer Composition: Deborah G. Tait (Manager),
    Monika D. Thayer, Janet Barnes Syring, Lillian Daniels

Design/Illustration: Antonio Alcalá, John Jackson,
    David Neal Wiseman
Photography/Illustration: Cover: Roger Foley, courtesy Antique
    Medley, Annandale, Virginia; 1: Roger Foley; 23: Clay tokens:
    Staatliche Museen zu Berlin, Preussischer Kulturbesitz,
    Vorderasiatisches Museum, photograph by Jürgen Liepe,
    1991. Coins, except Japanese and Chinese coins: The
    Smithsonian Institution, National Museum of American
    History, National Numismatic Collection; 47 *(lower right)*, 55
    (center and lower right), 63 *(top right)*, and 85 *(top right):* art
    by Yvette Watson
Overread: Barbara Klein

Consultant:
    Jon Eklund is curator of Physical Sciences and Computers
    and Information Technology at the National Museum of
    American History, Smithsonian Institution, Washington, D.C.

Library of Congress Cataloging-in-Publication Data
Inventions.
    p.   cm. – (A Child's First Library of Learning)
    Summary: Questions and answers explore the world of
inventions, explaining the creation of the radio,
toothpaste, and other modern necessities.
    ISBN 0-8094-9454-X
    1. Inventions–Miscellanea–Juvenile literature.
    [1. Inventions–Miscellanea. 2. Questions and answers.]
    I. Time-Life Books. II. Series.
T48.I53 1994
609–dc20   93-24417
                                     CIP
                                     AC

TIME-LIFE for CHILDREN ®

Assistant Managing Editors: Jean Burke Crawford,
    Patricia Daniels
Editorial Directors: Jean Burke Crawford, Allan Fallow,
    Karin Kinney, Sara Mark
Director of Marketing: Margaret Mooney
Publishing Assistant: Marike van der Veen

Original English translation by International Editorial Services
Inc./C. E. Berry

First printing. Printed in U.S.A.
Published simultaneously in Canada.

Time Life Inc. is a wholly owned subsidiary of
THE TIME INC. BOOK COMPANY.

TIME LIFE is a trademark of Time Warner Inc. U.S.A.

School and library distribution by Time-Life Education,
P.O. Box 85026, Richmond, Virginia 23285-5026.
For subscription information, call 1-800-621-7026.

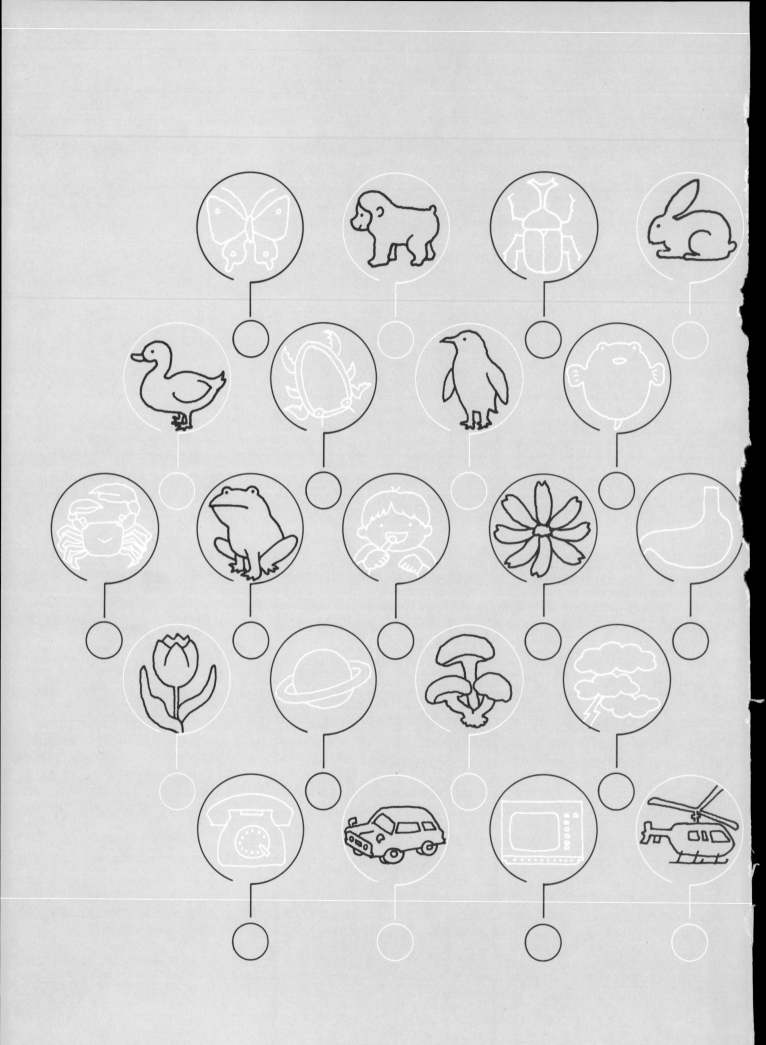